# More Than Weeds

# More Than Weeds

## L. Kiew

Nine
Arches
Press

**More Than Weeds**
**L. Kiew**

ISBN: 978-1-913437-64-0
eISBN: 978-1-913437-65-7

First published February 2023 by:

**Nine Arches Press**
Unit 14, Sir Frank Whittle Business Centre,
Great Central Way, Rugby.
CV21 3XH
United Kingdom

www.ninearchespress.com

Printed on recycled paper in the United Kingdom by:
Imprint Digital

Nine Arches Press is supported using public funding
by Arts Council England.

Supported using public funding by
**ARTS COUNCIL
ENGLAND**

# Contents

It's yours to walk the laid path's line or
stray past margins into wilds and beyond
or follow hints, seeds and references, it's yours
to see the wildflower meadow or a throng of weeds

# Psithurism

a woman walks into a city          there's a forest
of tall lights      concrete          high rise
        casts shadows          flecks the horizon

a woman walks into a city          there's a field
of tarmac      cars careen          windblown
         lights

street and lamp are intimate
     we could talk of crowds          not of lawn
        of congestion          or of overgrown grass

a woman walks into a city          there's an allotment
of people      uprooted          torn weeds     split seeds
        roadside tatters          far from windows

a woman walks into a city          there's one tree
        shattered          blossom      nubs of new
     she falls to her knees

         witness
how they bear the weight          every branch is a script
of bonegrip      on the earth          leaves spell
        the distances          slivers of hearts

# Tulips

here are the parks |              open to all
where they cherish      those companions
flowers                      if not all children |
where I thought     it would be different |
trusting |   |    |  |  people to be kind    |
where 54% are more likely to be     fined |
| commingling  | | | | we're      breaking  |
silence grows where stems harden | split |
1741 deaths |      | in custody |          bulbs |
are broken | |        all ways in this country |
and diagnosed  | |  disordered | |      plants
breaking  | |  colourstreaked  | | | | |       die
after being |  spat on |  newsprint's fragile |
petals blow apart     |       bleed underfoot |
we're not the virus  |      the flowers  dead |
in the earth                I cannot breathe
bodies more  |    |        than weeds |          |

# Knotweed

You loved me: furled leaves
tiger stalks and fleece flowers,
erect racemes on eager lips,
summer blooming cream and green.

I was triffidtender and how
bees loved us together,
the bamboo honey and
engorged lemony silence.

***

I put a knot in your stomach,
you say, I'm a house cancer.
I hate the way I can't hear
my name without spades ringing.

You cut and burn and
you bury what you burn.
I know I'm leaving something out.
Pesticides promise certainty.

I don't want this to be real.
I was hollowcored when Siebold
transported me to Holland.
My pain is in asphalt.

# Underground each word

fragments I speak are small
roots establishing in soil
along hedge banks
a leaf tilts to listen
when I speak again
the long line of roadside verges
montbretia blooms in late summer
I speak the breeze
through a plot of weeds

the Gardener forgot there are corms

through a plot of weeds
I speak the breeze
montbretia blooms in late summer
the long line of roadside verges
when I speak again
a leaf tilts to listen
along hedge banks
roots establishing in soil
fragments I speak are small

underground each word

# Ah Kong held our family together

Waking in the black hours
he sliced grooves
into tree every 20 seconds
then cycled miles from estate
to morning shift-school.
While the trees yielded milky latex
he tended these other saplings.
Tapping, he guided students'
calligraphy forming like treelace.

Then sun warmed everything.
Sap congealed in smallholder's cups,
white lumps for cents, salt, rice.
Days were long and still
his children couldn't eat until full.
An elastic band draws descendants
together. Monsoon comes,
mosquitos swarming
the rubbertapper's oil-lit lamp.

## Forest *text*

leaves through which *eyes and claws*
shoots and signs erupt *shape scrape*
word interrupt bark *and musang tails*
branches logograph *ideograms of fur*
in arching liernes *lagomorphs and*
foliole accumulate *tupai scat signs*
traces and rustling *cuneiform creeps*
rhizomes form *and sense squirles past*
green moans *in scratched script*
the forest voices *pen-tailed shrews*
its speech veridian *drunkenly scribes*
with ochre stripes *a musky notation*

# Ficus

In the time it takes a mynah
to alight, peck, defecate,
here I am: the seed tattoo,
hemiepiphyte under
the bark of her bough.

I germinate gently
smoothing aerial roots
in downward growth,
becoming a habit over
her brown-green trunk.

My epicotyls stroke her.
I sprout through her foliage
avid for rainkisses, sunshine.
We twine surcles, suckle
shadows, press together.

I coil from crown to soil.
I am shameless, clinging
roots in clefts, mossed forks.
I cradle her rhytidome
in my coarse basketwork.

I support her, shield her
from storms, hold her tighter.
She's precious, my hollowed core.
Murder takes all these years
and heart of my whole, she remains.

# Afterlife

Jáobholou, she'd had to go,
steerage rat on the iron boat
from Swatow; she'd refused again
and again to bind her feet.

Stubbornness landed her,
an old husband, nanyang,
their dry goods store, years
raising two sons, one not hers,
six daughters, grandchildren,
bhò-ĕng till the very last day.

\*\*\*

To hold her hand is to hold iron.
Laomà's palms are restless.
She forges a railroad from room to room.
Stationed she makes pomelos flower,
peeled segments fragrant.
Outside orchids overflow pots.

When Niutāo and Bhèming call,
she escapes under the back door
along the yellow wall, scurrying
grey and fast into the lalang –

# Corydalis lutea

She tries to breathe, balance
blooms like crested larks.
She's fled across walls to be
free as bluebells or narcissus.

Fumitory disguises her yellow.
By mid-Summer she's fernlike.
Her leaves are bleeding
hearts, groundcover for shade.

On poor soil she and her sisters
set roots and rhizomes.
To remain cheerful she believes
persistence rewards a place.

When she has a wasp in her mouth
she asks: can weed be just another
name the rain calls down
for refugee, unforced flower.

# Splits and rasps

Splits. Stilted. Silted. Salah tongue unrooted.
Re-rooting in cracked clay. Saliva fertile.
My tongue tills the earth, works. Seeds form.
Syllables tilted. Mana boleh? Bhò diót?

Touching tongues. Entwined vines. Wine
Tasting. Savoured saliva. Sa-lah. Recollect
idiolect. Sio:siot. Rasa saying. Slang.
Jàigiăng. Branching tongues routing.

Culvert. Tongue trying, overspills. Damn
my teeth. Tongue held back. Tongue released
a crop. Spitting out. Being spat out.
Being spat on. Lips missed, spot on.

# When we consider everything that grew

The highest and the lowest trees were the houses
of gods. Above us danced the tanager and
tinamou, the tyrannulet and trogon.
Feathers flashed bright blessings
as each bird flew, spreading seeds to sprout
green everywhere under our feet.

There was no silence. Tongues of leaves unfurled
songs to which lianas wound in counterpoint.
Epiphytes harmonised longing with orchids.
With their bark-breaths, trees chanted the names
of us, full of passionflowers and ferns
fronds' hymns to our community.

Sky drew our trees close enough to touch.
Ceiba placed arms tenderly around our mothers.
Our fathers rested without any fear
of brittleness in their broad branches.
Jaguar purred, stretched out on boughs.
Pudú and tamadou foraged among foliage.

We all thrived. In season there was always fruit,
soursop and maypop dropped into our hands.
Along the banks where water overlapped,
fish and snake quietly communed.
Quindío palms grew fat with rains,
thrust supple and tangled roots into soil.

The logger's axe made ghosts of us.
Our thoughts split like stems. We heard nothing
as articulate as wind in the wet canopy.
No trees to buttress us,
our steps are spores dispersed.
Our lips crack from asking why.

These edgelands are twigs, dust and
dust smothers us, stings skin and eyes,
evergreen only in memories, constant
pain so far from our trees we know.
Never to return, how can we remember
who we are, dabs and dots, faded colours.

# Lassaba

if I come to visit     calling her name
from the other side of the locked gate
       would she whisper back
while unhooking the rusted padlock

with the lightest of touches   no more
than a moth's white sweep on my arm
       would she usher me in

if I come   and stay the night
my parents on expedition upriver
       would she remain by me

      would her hand stop on my ankle
as a cloud pauses over the moon
against a dim bulb    paper wings
filling the hall with their shadows

## Seated lady x Ivy-leafed toadflax
## (x Aubrey Beardsley)

a snapdragon face reads exotic
          round to heart-shaped
her leaves alternate along
          thin stems winding silks
intricately the way a devil's ribbon
          weaves through brick

pollinated this mother of thousands
          turns photophobic
seams stone and concrete
          tendrilling down
to seed the underplaces
          overgrown with dark

it's so wet nestled and
          germinating in crevices
her daughters rustle
          shimmering over walls
their love for the sun is
          hot-soiled and naked

# Red rearranged

I pray for rain to wash away the paint
slashes on railings, bench and my palms,
note that red, its insistence
exists independent of my bewilderment.
Flowers and fruit come together with the marks
on a cheek, bloodstained teeth, nose rearranged.
Meanwhile a solitary chaffinch harmonises
with the penetrating chorale of traffic.
Tiny snails trail a map of regret and I can't
keep sitting here, counting shells.
His name was Rufus. I watch my cigarette burn.
One day I'll forget I have lost anything.

# Of rust, smut and mould

We encounter Norm as soon
as snow is gone from ground
at the earliest and lowest leaves.
Summertime he crouches
in a grove of corn, curious
over stem and footstalk.
He meditates bunt-ear,
blight, dust-brand, white
mildew, tawny snuff, spores,
standing cluster-cups.
He's close to the end
of a fostering plant,
seeing delicate threads,
a forest of filaments
flickering with breath.

# Impatiens glandulifera

we've spread since we first set in 1839
introduced as ornamental jewelweed
there've been a great many enthusiasts

Miss Welch who in 1948 collected
ripe pods from Sheffield and
transported us to the Isle of Wight

Mrs Norris of Camberley gave us
dripping pink to passers-by
our sticky seeds sedimenting shoes

thickets of us clog streams
we mass the banks of rivers
press damp together and splay in woods

now when they see us
lining green along roadsides
they let the Council know

we disperse aggressively they say
seed heads exploding after
noon showers puddle grass

unabashed we keep growing
mourning our mown sisters
not allowed forgiveness

we proliferate too seductively
for effective control and anyway
bees prefer us to the natives

between our roots we hold taut
and trusting as we first were
innocent seedlings from soil

# Rhubarb

ear-deep
amid the petioles
engorged and pink

listening
to the rain striking
a timpani of leaf-blades

my eardrums
itch after that slither
adder crowning the rhubarb

its hissing
wire-brushes my cochlea
crimson stalks

# Migrant

Under a flat stone, half log
or loose bark, frost-free and
not too wet, we are in torpor.
Days etiolate. We emerge,
most active in wet weather.
Subsisting, we squat and
exercise our tongues. Our pads itch.
A cold snap. We hesitate until night,
shuffle across fields and roads
to join the converging congregation
in our exodus towards the Ponds.
The males hop first. Some head
straight for weed-laced water;
others jostle the edges for Venus.

# Swallow

Grammars gather on powerlines.
Verbs twitter in the mangifera.
I roost in humid shade,
overeating from the dictionary –
nouns sticky as langsat,
a kilo of adjuncts, a kati of adverbs.

    uà ài: gāt lèu dǎ: jek dǎ ue

| orotund | nullibiety | opaque |
|---------|------------|--------|
| smeasling | desuetude | spoilage |

    uà ài: gāt lèu dǎ: jek dǎ ue

| minatory | plangent | deliquesce |
|----------|----------|------------|
| lutulent | sportive | grackle |

The words I swallow become
feathers poking through my skin.
I am fledging for the migration.
A window yawns,
a line of lipstick
palms reddening the horizon.

# Learning to be mixi

(i)

It was so panas
but aircon in airport
bite like cat.
Mother wave goodbye at gate
and
I was buckled in, and taken off
to England, the boarding school
(not like Enid Blyton, not at all) and
Cambridge, the colleges,
the backs and the hate,
suppressing the suffix-lah,
being proper and nice, cutting
my tongue with that ice.

(ii)

Ah Kong love learning-lah,
every day
reading Sin-Chew-Jit-Poh,
give his grandchildren all good
name: Hsueh Hui, Hsueh Zi,

call my brother lazy worm
for not reading book
but
when we came home
we left the chill,
Shakespeare at passport control,
filled our ears with warm tones,
jiat hò a bhue?

(iii)

When I took my Scots partner home
speaking proper English, he asked
"Honey, di'ye ken ye jest switched
tongues mid-sentence."
Dialect like a blush licked
my face, campur-campur
speech bursting the ice wall,
jopuēt: puēt ue

# Self-portrait as Bartlett pear

Pausing
I consider
me fat
slightly
disfigured
heavy-hipped
and the pear, its honey
juice scenting all fingers.
An early child, my parents found
me awkward. I know a fruit now
can be the size of the world, and self-sufficient
without self-doubt, memory milks petals
the first to appear on the trees, blossom
filling the orchard with light.

# Gombak

Wet greeted us everywhere, its green
mossiness, earthy and insinuating between
flipflop and feet, woody drips from the dark
canopy, squelching leaflitter. It licked us
along the dark corridor, skidding from concrete
kitchen onto long veranda and down
the steep slope to that sudden sunlit
padang and beyond, flowing glints
clean water, swift, and there she was:

Sungai; kakak, capricious sister,
she sprayed us with sweet stream scent,
skirted soft sandstone, rocks slippery,
shoulders undercutting earth banks.
Her spirits altered after the rains.
Waking us, she grumbled gravel,
grumpy at being rust-rushed, bearing
the load of overlogging, heavy sediment
from up valley deforestation.

Our old white Ford was a rhino,
turning reluctantly out of the gate;
its lurch-lumber expelled me from
forest home to other study stations.
Tear-blind, feeling sick, evicted,
I looked back to the red-roofed
refuge of road-scarred lorrymen,
its altar offering oranges and incense,
the giant banyan with roots upward,
branches hunched over, weeping.

# Bakkwa

because we could never be home
for Chinese New Year     aunts gift
sticky squares of pork     box big
enough for eighteen airborne hours

because sesame     fish sauce
five spice heats          dídí's breath
and chilli coats        my tongue
because I am thirteen     and he's ten

because we can't eat it all
want something for the days ahead
because we lie     declare nothing at customs
we are stopped

# Chicken

Ah Ba said there was no refrigerator
when he grew up
if you didn't eat it
quickly
all at once
it went bad
or worse
someone else ate it

but
Mother was going to ration it
the whole week
sliced in sandwiches
saving for dinner
the carcass
bones picked clean
ready for soup

this is England 1983

how could he be
a mouth
always open

the emptied plate between them

how could she be
a cupboard
always locked

# Of the shortest day

What has survived is the belief
that water tastes best today;
the moon offers help through the dark.

What has survived is the memory,
pullut-rice rolled between palms,
ballcakes in pandan-ginger syrup.

What has survived is the custom,
serving girls even pairs,
adding strength to their futures.

What has survived is the altar
table lit by red candles,
joss paper burning in the iron pot.

What has survived is together
tasted on the tongue
as ancestors' faces fade in frames.

# Rabbits

When I see rabbits
glutting grass banks
by Inverness station
I think how fortunate
I am to live
among such abundance.

Laomà told me why
jade rabbit leapt
into ravenous flames.
She could eke out
an egg for eight mouths
with pigweed: dangiù jià u.

She marvels at fat
ducks in the public park
wonders at food
banks stacked with tins
recalls the savour of ants
snares being empty.

# Kuih Kapit

You saved sweetness in a Jacob's cracker tin
for when I came home. You started my heart
again in the kitchen with kopi, Dutch Lady milk
and kuih, the right shade of brown, not too pale,
not turning dark, each one moulded over
a charcoal brazier in our shaded backyard.
You told me how a Peranakan girl hid love
notes in her biscuits, threw each over the wall
for the boy next door and how his little brother
found them and told everyone their secrets.
I wondered why you never married. We both
have little brothers. Today it's cold and dark,
the biscuits shop-bought. I eat them alone
and anxious after the taste of sugar if I stop.

# Testimony against Robert Fortune and his ilk

zealous collectors of scant morality you assert
your right to everything
xylem bleeds and it was you
who confined us in Wardian cases
vain is your acquisition and            in vain you exclude those
unprofitable                            our sisterweeds see to that
tame smooth and subdue as you like
shades of trees yield nothing       we're not bounded
roots forced in quest to
quicken the mercantile economy    wriggle free
planttrapper seedthief you see
empty ground ripe for resettlement and you
not only claim but frame soil in cold
measures of demise domain dominion
lawn is a penitentiary and your false
knowledge imposed
just to make you gleamrich
it is so much chaff

                                   hearts here are
                                   groundswelled flowers flowers
                                   flowers from bulbs and shoots
                                   emerging shy saplings heal
                                   disturbance of earth spadebroken
                                   calm is the foliage
                                   beyond threat of hand axe mower
                                   and we grow

# How the tree feels

If you're going to stop, greet
a favourite tree with a pat
and a cheery "alright bud"
on your walk to the station, consider

are you like the spinose suited director
brambling the greenest secretary
as she stands barktight, photocopying.
Traffic swallows silence.

A solitary sparrow, followed by
another, then a trio tweets
their arrival in the twigs
above. They saw you do it.

# Rhododendron

Nothing short of calling in the army
will put things right. Too many are rooted
here, their lateral growth occupying hillsides.
Police repeatedly rescue walkers
from stinging branch-cages, their bodies
sap-smeared contract dermatitis.

Windborne stealth-seeds
germinate in their millions.

We've tried horses and chains to rip them
from the soil, have cut limbs and
dowsed their trunks with herbicide.
Even after forced removals
a deep layer of toxic mulch remains.
We must start again.

# Open gardens

*after Kona Macphee*

my people pass

                                                      abandoned wastelands

              stop to dig and stake
              sift soil into clean beds

my people use
              earthsplattered tools
              a day at a time

                                                        plants wild around ruins

and my people overlook

                                                    catmint and cardoons
                                                    the rough corners
                                                    riotous with nettles and snails

my people tolerate

                                                    fat hen and pig thistle

       hands propagate
       tongues enjoy

my people thrive
              deadhead and pot            green
              into ordered clumps

my people begin to root out

                                                    abrasive colours

                                                    among the casualties
                                                    bearded iris red phlox

my people unfold dark
                    dirt dreams of tendrillling
                                        winddrifts of pollen
                    cultivars bearing bright heads


when my people rise
how easy it becomes
                to fence what grows
                            to put closed signs on the gates

# Buddleja davidii

What is my own      name?  not that one
the French-Basque missionary's and me
from Sichuan uprooted me      collected
catalogued          cultivated in foreign

soil  What is my      name?      commonly
escaped from gardens      listed invasive
labelled noxious weed  What is my own
                  name?   wind-sown

making a home in        dry open ground
cracks in bricks by roadsides    building
sites and in the          aftermath of war
on bombsites          broken   railway lines

What is my own      name?   grows into
thicket   butterfly bush      summer lilac
bees' amah    shrub   vigorous I own and
am arching   I name myself        perfect

# Rust Square

too-still July
lies in the brown grass
city castaway

on this heat island
she and trees are stressed
the sky is empty

on the ground
everywhere beetles
husks beechmast

has she noticed
the acorns are green
falling too early

# We've taken Rosa

We're not asking for a lot                    only what we need and
we're as serious as brown thrips        Don't tell the Head Gardener
Rosa's staked         stems tied with twine        somewhere
you won't find her                          She's delicate

twigs like fingers        torn from a  hand        It will be
simple to pry        her red buds apart        deflower
We won't unbind her                  until you give us
the mulch that is ours        Do this        We're watching

We hope for composure        that it doesn't rain today
If there's a slightest frondstir        on the compost heap
we'll trash her naked    of leaf        thin her to
strangulated shoots        strung like a fence

We have secateurs                and will sever
We'll    handle    the situation    A    spade's    a    spade
Believe    we are blowndark        our tongues
thornedged    We won't be kept out    of direct light

# Wisteria

Mr Reeves said the vigour of the plant
makes her adaptable
makes her trainable to many forms

he said bind her tight and break
side shoots back to basal
Mr Reeves didn't say

he transported
her seedlings          a stealing a separating
soil forked shovelled raked

                    the sound of it
                    anything but
her soft stem around any available support

said maturation forced by physically
abusing the main trunk
Mr Reeves said root pruning

brings an abundance
of purple                          I count
                                   each cutting

# On being told by police

I can't remember; just walls, wet, in the house at the edge of the field
red flowers in the shade of the wall

       red rose petals among the stones
                  ragdoll in a heart-shaped dream

               open
                  did I open
                        at the entrance someone

                                don't
                                pinch
      outside wild thyme and the bottom of my  pocket torn; this isn't over
              it's still occurring;  I don't remember

did I whisper a warning to myself, to someone else
don't go on
don't go any further, I don't remember
                coming in
       he was coming down the stairs, the tread light and fast, almost
       running; the sound was like spring rain

                        did I run; did he follow me in
               don't
     I am coping; my skin is a border crossing; there were hedges and a fat robin
     singing; the opposite of a warning

red rose petals among the stones
               ragdoll in a heart-shaped dream

don't worry, the roses; the womb's a solitary cocoon; will it be a red admiral
                          I can't remember
                footsteps; no one coming in

did I whisper, rose,  run, run, run

remember


swallows nesting, seen through the open window; the room wasn't occupied
stanchions of dark wet stone like a black back hunched under an umbrella


open

did I open


red slipper, doll
   abandoned
      coming in, too huge, and the rough stones by my head; I don't remember


don't

anyone, please
cold wet stone


did I hear footsteps; I can't remember; the rain light on petals


did I


wet ragged petals, ooze circles, foul a pool
black swallow worrying flies in the air through the field


red rose rags on the stones
cold wet doll, all muddled
I don't remember

open

did I

open

# In search of

*after C.D. Wright*

under frugal moons I abandon     myself to slope
I like to eat strawberries     with salt
I have firm hips and a shedding     stoop
my favourite fruit is stone     we could rehome
snails from the allotment     it's not their fault
they're migrant     I'll meet you by the gingko trees
shells seem impenetrable but all     you need
is an egg tooth     I don't remember where I was
when Diana died     snakeshead fritillaries seem
perfect for bridal bouquets     I have plenty
of thyme   don't turn compost     let's subside
I wish (like earthworms) we left casts     aren't
the cornflowers astray?     I could always fall into
bed  if I could     I would use only terracotta pots
the rat infestation drew a fox     just yesterday
small bones are crunchiest white     if we're going
to dig  let's dig right here     earth mounds have
great potential     three winters I wore green
woollen masks a yellow scarf     my second cousin
hand-pollinates     the neighbours call him Bumble
it's the truth that germinates at blood temperature
that's cute  right?  I'm ready   I'll try crossbreeding

## You who treat desire like an app on your phone

know that I am sister to nightshade,
eve-open for attraction of moths.
In company my leaves may be fetid
with bruises but my calyx throws off
a powerful perfume all summer.

O now you fall quiet and crave
comfort of peanut butter, dog's nose
and voice notes. You try to swipe
away but listen, listen, those scraping
breaths are spiny seedpods

rattling ears in wind. This thornapple
woman curses you. Know the signs.
It's too late to be wishing
every hole is your friend. Wet
grass slurs juicy with worms.

You end frequenting roadsides
halfway between wall and verge,
root in soil rank with the refuse.
Your heart fails. Me, I dream
a fettling, moon-white trumpets.

# Boscage

He takes my hand and takes me
into the garden to see his topiary
balls, viridescent and rustling.
Sunlight touches my thigh
quietly, here and here while
rootlets scritch damp bulbs,
tempting under swells of soil.
His hands part low branches,
spread twigs, show me
the hungrier of heart, their furred wriggling;
so many caterpillars are stripping
green tissue, denuding stems.
Unpinned silk and a flash of white
triangle edged in purplish-brown,
box-moth takes flight.

# Postcards

I saw this and thought of you.
Do you remember the red caps,
searching under one for a face
that'd look like Shakespeare's?

I think of you still peering
behind flowerpots, at the back
of charity shops. I'm weeding
beds and borders for inspiration.

I saw this Major's garden
ornament. He's nearly all Bard,
full of supposition, conjecture.
Perhaps the writing is always hard.

You remember how we loved
that craze for travelling gnomes?
The Ann Atkin collection is
in storage. You could have stayed.

I saw this gardenalia today.
Didn't you have one of these?
I keep the heart you gave me
in the old potting shed.

I thought of you and saw this.
Have you found what you were
looking for? Do remember
it's cold outside. Keep well.

# Planatus x hispanica

Rain has flushed thought
as dust off five-pointed leaves.
Drops chatter beyond the dripline,
seep into the underground springs
that Tradescant's natural hybrids
stand over like green sentinels.
How marvellous: each tree capable
of sucking up 500 gallons a day
keeping London's clay from heave,
the shallow circumference,
roots netting the ground level.
Men used to grow watercress
where now there's dry lawn.
Improbable. What might root next?

# She's against thieving

Through bamboo slats, the sun
bakes stripes on grey concrete. Next door
fruit bats sleep uneasily in the eaves.

Francesca squats behind the open kitchen,
cuts *The Star*, *The Straits Times*
into paper squares. She makes ready,
waits for the day to back away
to a steaming horizon.
Its rice-porridge heat cools,
condensation on dark grass.
At seven o'clock Francesca rises,
straightens her samfu to climb
the long-armed tree that crouches
breeding shade in the corner of our yard.

One by one she wards each
not-yet-ripe green head
with words she cannot read.

## When the tattooist says I sat
## like a rock all day, I think

of  the  water        parting        around me
drenched granite      plumes of weeds    flashfin
of trout      the stickleback   and      a quick green
spatter        frog   dunking    from a high dive

of the moorhen        muddling midstream
and otter      decanting        out of the beck
basking   as is its right        in the love of the sun
irradiated spray   teeth   like needle points

of midday       afterburn      my tattooed calf
how water continues    eddying around what was sunk
withholding     submersing       how I'm hurt
and the willow leaning in       strokes my face

# Karwinski's fleabane

Thank you for collecting me. I know now
I was uncultivated and
I wasn't any good against fleas.
You forgave me,
called me dependable daisy,
let me soften edges, carpet stony ground.
Thank you for giving me a bed
in the rockery, the slivers of space.
You appreciated how I bloomed,
white-arrayed for most of the summer.

It seems I've outgrown your welcome,
no longer fitting the floral scheme
spilling from understorey and
onto driveway, wrinkling roots
into the tiny gaps I discover.
I've heard you talking about me:
prolific self-seeder, easy
to kill and difficult to keep out.
You gouge clumps, scorch
earth and spray glyphosate.

I know you are busy. Thank you
for not committing enough
effort to root me out.
My petals uncurl. I'm settled
and my seedlings sprawl out.
I love seaside, small cracks.
I hate hard winters.
Pioneer of disturbed sites
I remain grateful
for the wind, the part sun.

# If I'd gathered enough or held you

a mermaid's purse lightly attached to weed
maybe there would have been no cramping
or tides bearing away the floating foam

or if I'd fallen asleep sitting up maybe
I could have clutched you safe despite
a precarious nest on the basalt ledge

maybe if I'd been a cave swiftlet building
a saliva-cup of stringy vegetation sticking
secure to walls if we hadn't been prey

maybe if there'd been no buffeting
no white shock if I'd had the strength
pale fingernails clawing rock or if crying

I'd have caught you before the fall maybe
I'd have felt your heart or seen your eyes
instead of black wings beating

maybe if I'd not been cracked or
salt-crusted a shell releasing red
love maybe I'd have been enough

# Francesca

who stood
ready at one o'clock

with fried rice on a plate
and Yeo's tomato ketchup

who makes sweet
and sour pork better than anyone

who taught me
how to peel prawns and boil

the shells to inhibit their smell and
civets from coming to the backyard

who tends
the avocado tree, who picks its fruit

who showed me chicken feathers
snakeskin feet, choppered its head

draining rich ruby into
a bowl, coagulating

who walks to church
daily, strong as bamboo

who lives on the hill,
is persistent

# Phyllotaxis

1.
don't talk to the street trees

they aren't from here

implants
interlopers
imports                                   from over there
crowd   out the pavements
rooting in British soil
stop        penetrating the turf


1.
at city borders
immigrants    wait in groves          standing

stretching out their limbs
for rain's inspection


2.
the flags         blooming
boils on white-washed walls

petals spiral                      scatter
criss-crossing    roadways

are handkerchiefs
are sighing doves


3.
never enough     sun
no matter

where we put down
roots

5.

redrosebuds
pursed tight
disapproving
those mouths

rosette
    on rare days
when it's bright
                enough
                she opens up

bees come visiting
outside welcomed in

8.

leylandii demarcations
flanking the running
drains green-black shades

        car driving away
        roots burlapped
        boxes bound
        string one left
        transient

13.

wind
spindrift      against      opposing barricades
                                rearrangements

21.

always teenagers     trespassing
                    breaking bounds
                    walking
trees in a gale
as numerous as refugees


34.

growing towards each other
                  shyness
                        an edge of blue
                tender  not quite crowning


55.

alien         incursion
                    whispered
                    disappeared
                    in the localised
        area
                    streets darken into forest


89.

fungus        grips with blackened fingers
woundstump tips      barkstripped seize
   scattered arms         uprooted feet
brokebacked bole          castrated
fired         twigs     ashashashashash
harm        held    to the sun

        don't look don't speak don't
        soil don't wait don't hibernate
        run go elsewhere runrunningrunrun

144.

pollen
settles
on skin

irritant

rogue
shedding
bark

invasiveinvasive
migrantweed

spreads
seedlings

root them out
dig over the grounds

233.

displaced copse
dance of litter leaves
unacclimatised shadows

furrowing the dirt
bitterness that has
no descendants

377.

ghostleaf

carbondioxide in
oxygen out

breathstirred

broken
open
flame

foreign seed
germinates

# Do not trust

quiet kept by high fences      lawn's
genteel regimen    this is not for you
stems temporarily tolerated  around
garden benches     flowers detained
in damp beds          for two months
less than a season     know a peony
may be staked          for 1002 days
a seeding point  the undocumented
don't fall easily    to fork and trowel
it isn't like concrete    never cracks
and wind carries      discriminately
trust a bare minimum              soil
shelters seedlings              in place

# Vandals

there are green invaders
among mothers with bugaboo prams
toddlers scattering bread
not quite in range of the ducks

parakeets are sacking city trees
squawking over the grey suited
workers with pecking entourages
pigeons scavenging for crumbs

they're feral flashmobs
raiding suburban bird tables
noisome and eating all
the sunflower seeds and nuts

it's no wonder that magpie
on its beat like a policeman
with powers to stop and search
calls them hooligans – says

Send      Them      Back

# St Anthony's fire

is formed of      incorrupt
tongue or        just for eating
I run and grassy-heave
itch fragile as geraniums

the breeze is lying    I don't listen to it
downpath I avoid the susceptible
grasses      brush and burst spores
check me    has bleeding stopped

sphagnum overflowing pockets
I hold hard to notebook and
pencil stubs       can I do nothing
rotate crops   avoid cockspur

not inclined to spasms and seizures
I pray for clean farm-saved seeds
but grains are windtossed silence
husks        unhitch from earth

# When I said I wanted to be

*after Leila Macdonald*

Rose what I meant was
I wanted to be that girl prettily
poised at the prow of an ocean liner
ship's wake white behind her
arms opened wide
and nobody surprised
at her        embracing the totality

And now?        I know who I am
not cultivated like roses
drooping        in vases
I am rattan        unsplit cane
nothing decorative        brown spines
strong        climbing        with grace

# Geoxyle

Words spark the silence
yet nothing's been said
about the sun's smother,
its hardening spread.
Of savannah, tall grasses.
How to search for forest
is to walk its canopy.
The red wings catch.
Now flames. Deafening.
Earth blackening, breaks.
Trees avoid damage
in the dark. What happens is
what happens. Names learnt.
Sand apple. Plough breaker.

# Robinia pseudoaccacia

In this place woodmen crack smiles
behind backs of fleshy hands
while axeing saplings.

Outside plantation I live
no stranger, sucker-spread,
re-grow when cut down and spiny.

I stand kin to false, the feral
in disturbed areas
spill flowers in a downrush.

The other trees and me stay silent,
stretch haphazard canopies and
listen for robins, bees and rain.

# Voices I have not heard

*after Alice Meynell*

The woods are tarred with roads and
piled everywhere seraya logs,
brushstrokes across orange ground.

There is no birdsong, no sound
of serow rootling after seeds,
no proboscis monkey calls.

Silence is the only blossom.
The rafflesias are long vanished
and dusk canopies the hills.

In leftover light a leaf curls,
desiccated tongue
for what I haven't found.

# Intent

the field
edge dumpland
seems unaware until I trip
over a stick and then every plant knows
me tiny among tumuli and drifts of my litter
I grope the wasteland bearing paleness of moon
on fingernails little bones thrown glass and plastic
I hear brittle taproots bulbs breaking and spreading


      o      o      o


when the rain arrives
it is so insistent
she is coming
      field edger   cereal killer   weed witch
hot spots we created         are her holy places
greenhouse gas           is her invocation
      Striga beautiful invader
all plants move         we move them

# Gleditsia tricanthos

Tree turning orange-gold
hangs huge seedpods
offering honeyed pulp
with so much love but
my mouth is full of shadows
rough and scaley when I swallow.
Father is buying a funeral.

I remember leaves late spring
emerging lime and pinnate.
Leaflets harden to darker green.
The sun parched open crowns.
Zig-zag thorns snag and
scars grew over smooth.
I squat, broken soil

and old bark at back is strange
and as familiar as my skin.
I too am yellowed,
trying to slough off
rejection like rain.
In these green-veined times
Father wants to be prepared.

# The more I tasted the more I understood

each June to August      I am drawn as are
dog-faced bats to heavy-sweet flowers    and
tigers and elephants to split-spiked shells
hungry for civet-pungent cleads          aromatic
creamy seeds and                  longing to be home to eat
outside by roadside stalls        sticky-handed
squatting on the back porch        sweating lightly

my tongue cries on                palate scent-snagged
for Chook Kiok Musang King bittersweet D24
anosmia is an aching              I feel always
the shucked shell of home                    and how
when eating's ended              with it
the chance to stay                        and here I am
thrown far from the tree      a thorn-crowned rind

unwelcome as the durian on public transport
again and again          having to politely explain
to nose-holders          the perfumed enticement
the endozoochory          what I crammed in my stomach
what is dispersed          unruly and incongruent
in this scentless city          on bleached streets    at court
segmented      (at least that's how I feel)          split open

# Only in the interest of national security

*The Home Secretary decides each case personally.*
         moon turns away
         cucumbers are shivering
         who likes the trellis and the stake
the Gardener prunes and harrows   leaves bone-whitened
         first fellings    thin trailings
*Though we will always try to tell an individual*
*that their citizenship is to be deprived*
         how fast fronds fall to soil
*it might not be possible in exceptional circumstances.*
the fog leans in     dripping insinuations
         even though we've been here
         before and for a long time
         we're only hedge clippings
*Because we cannot immediately tell a person*
*that they are to be deprived of British citizenship*
fog is one wet slap after another
         to the fallen   leaves returned
*it does not make the decision any less valid*
*or prevent the deprivation order being made.*
         dandelions in dirt
         plastic zip-ties   twine
*Process and safeguards are already in place.*
         on wind's moan
         a slam shut   sound
         may be left   human
*We would explain their appeal rights when*
*they make contact with us.* how the ground lies
         lillies pretend to know
         nothing of it
the Gardener grows more shadows   grows more
         silence   how are we to bear
         branches left for crows

# There's always spontaneous combustion

Greasy shadow was all I remained
cold on the slab of pavement
where cracks gaped large enough
for names to slip and be lost.
Silence was sudden, an absence
of traffic on the always-busy road
and ashes scattered, blown off
barely dowsed, burned bones.

Did you wonder where the fire came from?
It had been a hot summer, and stress
made everywhere a good place to build
a pyre. For hungry ghosts, laughter
crackles and eyes strike the lines
swifts carve in light, that white haze.
We creep inexorably to flash point.
Word is *the world can catch fire*.

Fraxinella in the herbaceous border
sweats isoprene against the heat.
Today swelters volatile with oils.
I haunt the walls, watch sparrows
peck apart a parched worm.
It's never been easy to speak,
tongue tinder dry in mouth,
teeth ready to grind sparks.

# We remember when blood and love were just

i.

unsettled gusts              we were brushed past
as if we'd shared                  five hundred
dirty lovers                       was it just?

shops shuttered           how people looked
concrete creviced      heads turned eyes slitted
hands as rough          and the taken away

how it wasn't enough     dried seeds bartered
65g of our blood       not saying their names
for one egg           how each was broken

we felt the sun as         the wind carried
tender fern             spores from place
easily dispersed              to place

ii.

how the trees were rooted   and we spoke nothing
barely yes    trees were born of peace    xiǎo kang
the months that abundance       taking a long time
days to sprout slow from soil         and it was vital
to breathe and keep breathing  strong and strange
until it felt like    we    might    drift    break    off
and float as leaves    gathering in mounds at night
not saying anything about that    sap couldn't clot
and we were within      microns       of the perfect
distance from each other     sky ten coughs above
and the wind two metres away    squirrels outside
seemed to stand and say     life is a simple matter
more or less to lick a tree until      a tongue is sad

# These trees were considered beautiful

*10,000 planted in Bermondsey*

What have I learnt? Trees of heaven are
allelopathic, extend out of neglected heaps,
gratings, cement. They burgeon
from both their seeds and cut roots.
I take dropped flowers home.

Mother warns me, her good-for-nothing
stump-sprout, we're like these trees –
if too resilient, thriving just about everywhere,
we'll be seen one day as too many
ghetto palms struggling to reach the sky.

Anger like a wind threads between gaps
in tubular railings and across waste ground.
May chòuchūn spread out, suckering vigorously.
May they continue to grow semen-scented
panicles erect above heart-scarred canopies.

# Today everything is on fire

the wind claws
crimson back & forth

running across grass

trees catch
leaves ember & cinders

***

I pray
please rain
save some green

there's a grasshopper
poised for flight
at the bottom of the page

# The conservator

The bomb and what happened after.
Charlock and clover grew after.
Among the rubble she picked after
glister. Bellis perennis persisted after
war opened spaces. Lucerne came after
and fireweed flamed unbroken.

Wild flowers were hopes after.
She compressed those after
and between flimsy sheets. After
the blast, she pressed leaves after
leaves, petals into an ever after
of absorbent blotters. She lived

to preserve. She was feeling after
something. Nothing was white after.
She stored specimens after
drying. Foliage labelled after
a taxonomy of loss. And after
that she put seeds in packets.

# Weeds are wild

not of the garden cast | out in the wrong places along
the verge | the air palpably dense weeds are at
boundary of houses | at the bottom of lawns weeds
wish for completeness of night | weeds lie in tree pits
fill your dreams with yellow glow | weeds are petal and
leaf push up in patterns and here's a shape that could
be a body | weeds are disappearing to get changed |
weeds attract butterflies| bees listen to weeds | weeds
are trusting | follow you like a lover's caress along
instep | hem | calf | the thigh | weeds have long stems
from root to tip brown-skinned | hairy buds | are what
to yank what to leave and what you should never touch
| weeds are itching | to be perfect | weeds are asking
for it | weeds interfere and are common cannot be
confined | weeds' answer is in blooming | blessings
bruise under the cheekbone | vile | weeds are a four
year wait for justice | weeds are abandoned | sprout
tongues randomly while there's room for languages to
grow | there's no need to pull weeds | to get rid of
weeds check first how they testify | stalked yellow a
part ripped away too coarse to spread | missing
fingernails | a circle of swallowed quiet | weeds you
thought you'd pulled quietly continue creeping | weeds
claim more | weeds still | won't be enough | weeds are

# To live here

*after Paul Éluard*


The door slammed. I tended a fire,
a crackling of acer leaves,
a bonfire of flaming herberis,
camellias, azaleas, living flames.

I gave what the garden gave:
shrubs, sycamore, long grass,
white-faced houses, wooden
benches, laughter from the shade.

Into the conflagration I flung
myself, petals, language
drifting from the page, not
belonging, longing to live. Here.

# Seeding and sproutings

The page is an open fertile space in which to explore. I am a grubby speaker, imperfect and imperfectly multi-lingual. I feel no need to set borders between this language and that. My poems twine with and alongside the other poets' propagations and language plantings.

I do not italicise words because none of them are 'other', 'exotic' or 'foreign' to me; I grew up moving constantly between them. While English is the language of my education, a fact that owes much to colonialisation, it is just one of the languages I speak.

Poetry proliferates along the edges, whether of the raised bed of meaning or friable soil of sense. It bears fruits and flowers, both for the ear and for the eye. I believe that all communication is to some extent partial and problematic; and poetry is to me one of the least dogmatic of the artforms. It is landscaped as much by the reader as the poet.

I also believe that readers are curious and able to enjoy the sounds and shapes of words, to dig out meaning from context, and to explore using the many tools and resources are available online.

I branch between English and Teochew most often in my poems; the Southern Min language is spoken by Teochew people in the Chaoshan region of eastern Guangdong and by the diaspora around the world. The variant I speak has been seeded through migration with loan words from Bahasa Malaysia and other Chinese languages, most often Hokkien and Cantonese.

There are several different romanization schemes for Teochew. Standard written Chinese is based mainly on Mandarin and adapted for use by other Chinese languages. Because I don't read and write Chinese characters fluently, I have chosen to use a pinyin-based transliteration system; it might be more familiar to readers who come to Chinese languages via Mandarin. While I use the free English-Teochew dictionary and phrasebook *WhatTCSay* app, all errors and inconsistencies in transliteration and tone marks are mine. I am grateful to its developers Ty Eng Lim and Khiem Lam, and all gaginang.

# Horticultural notes and numbers

Of the plant hunters, botanical raiders and bio-pirates appearing in the poems, their histories and exploits are easily found.

'Only in the interest of national security': Title and text in italics are from Policy paper: *National security and Borders Bill: Deprivation of Citizenship Factsheet*, published 3 December 2021.

'These trees were considered beautiful': A favourite of social reformer, Ada Salter and the Bermondsey Beautication Committee, these Ailanthus altissima were planted as the frontline of an urban-environmental revolution under the slogan of "Fresh air and fun".

'Phyllotaxis': The poem's numbering reflects the Fibonacci sequence. A version of the poem exists as an interactive Bitsy computer game created in collaboration with Michael Weston. Play it at:
http://www.lhhkiew.co.uk/games/phyllotaxis.html
Thanks to Nick Murray for his inspiring Artblab talk on poetry and computer games.

About the statistics in 'Tulips' and 'Do not trust': in 2020, the figures in 'Tulips' were among many quoted in news articles. The UK has no statutory upper time limit on the period that an individual can be held in immigration detention. At the time of writing 'Do not trust', the person who had been in immigration detention for the longest had been detained for close to three years. See for current detention figures: https://migrationobservatory.ox.ac.uk/resources/briefings/immigration-detention-in-the-uk/

# Acknowledgements

I am grateful to the editors of the following publications in which some of these poems or versions of them first appeared: *Amberflora, Bad Lillies, Beardsleyque, Crossing lines* (Broken Sleep anthology), *Domestic Cherry, Fenland Reed, Fenland Poetry Journal, Finished Creatures, Harana, Haverthorn, Ink Sweat & Tears, Intersectional Geographies* (exhibition catalogue, Martin Parr Foundation), *LossLit, Molly Bloom, New Voices Rise* (London Library anthology), *Poetry Salzburg, Poetry Wales, Pollux, The Rialto, Shearsman, Smoke, Stand, Tears in the Fence, The Dark Horse, The Projectionist's Playground, The Scores, The Selkie, Umbel and Panicle, Under the Radar, Wasifiri.*

'When we consider everything that grew' was commissioned by Hayward Gallery for the *Among the Trees* exhibition. 'To live here' was featured as part of the Royal Society of Literature's Write Across London project.

I thank Martha Sprackland and everyone at Offord Road Books for publishing my pamphlet, *The Unquiet* (2019) in which some of these poems or earlier versions appears.

Many poets have given me inspiration and feedback as I worked towards this collection. In particular I am grateful for these communities: the Saturday Group poets past and present including Jennifer Wong, Mary Robinson, Ann Pelletier-Topping, Joanna Ingham, Danne Jobin, Jinhao Xie, Tim Tim Cheng; Bi'an and the writers I spent time with in 2019 at the Arvon Centre course; 2018/2019 TOAST poets cohort; London Library Emerging Writers 2019/20 cohort and in particular Helen Bowell and Isabelle Baafi; Nur Khairiyah for Rumah Khai; Maisie Chan for Bubble Tea Writers; alice hiller for the Saying the Difficult Thing community; Poetry School Mixed Borders garden residency programme which was my gateway to London Gardens Trust, British horticulture and the urban green space movements; Astra Papachristodolou for Poem Atlas and Steven J Fowler for Poem Brut.

My thanks also to poets and teachers, Patience Agbabi, Alvin Pang, Miriam Gamble and Peter Mackay (Pàdraig MacAoidh).

Deepest gratitude to Jane Commane for her incisive editorship and supportive nurturing of my collection, as well as the Nine Arches Press team.

And finally, thank you to Michael Weston for his continuing support and love.